WHUT MAKES YOU THANK TEKSUNS TAWK FUNNY?

By Ken Rigsbee

Oak Hill Printing and Copy Center
Austin, Tx 78735   512-892-3762

Cover Design by Harry McCabe

Distributed by Cuerno Largo Publications

6406 Old Harbor Lane

Austin, Texas 78739-1547

PRINTING HISTORY

1st Printing - June, 1987
2nd Printing - August, 1987
3rd Printing - October, 1987
4th Printing - March, 1988
5th Printing - November, 1988
6th Printing - July, 1989
7th Printing - September, 1989
8th Printing - July, 1990
9th Printing - October, 1990
10th Printing - November, 1990
11th Printing - February, 1991
12th Printing - March, 1991
13th Printing - May, 1991
14th Printing - July, 1991
15th Printing - September, 1991
16th Printing - November, 1991
17th Printing - February, 1992
18th Printing - May, 1992
19th Printing - January, 1993
20th Printing - May, 1993
21st Printing - September, 1993
22nd Printing - July, 1994
23rd Printing - August, 1995
24th Printing - July, 1996
25th Printing - April, 1997
26th Printing - October, 1997
27th Printing - August, 1998
28th Printing - March, 2000
29th Printing - November, 2000
30th Printing - July, 2001
31st Printing - March, 2003
32nd Printing - February, 2004

ISBN 0-9615296-1-X

FORWARD — ACKNOWLEDGEMENT

Having lived and traveled extensively throughout the Southwest, I have enjoyed and made constant reference to the following sources in order to translate some of the native dialects into something which I understood:

1. "How to Speak Southern" by Steve Mitchell (Bantam Books, Inc.)
2. "The Illustrated Texas Dictionary of the English Language", Volumes I, II, III, IV, by Jim Everhart (Creative Books of Houston)

After living in Texas for a while I discovered that although Texans don't really talk "funny", some folks still seem to have trouble understanding them. Therefore, in the interest of serving humanity, I have attempted to include herein some of the most frequently misunderstood words and phrases in the "unofficial" language of Texas. I have referenced those which were first noted by the above authorities with subscripts corresponding to the numbers above — you see, sometimes they talk "funny" just like we do. Following each definition and example sentence I have shown the equivalent English word or phrase in parentheses (for the benefit of any foreigners who might need them).

This booklet is dedicated to the several secretaries and many associates who have had to struggle with the "funny" way I say things.

Ken Rigsbee
Sugar Land, Texas

The Grayte State uh TEKSUS

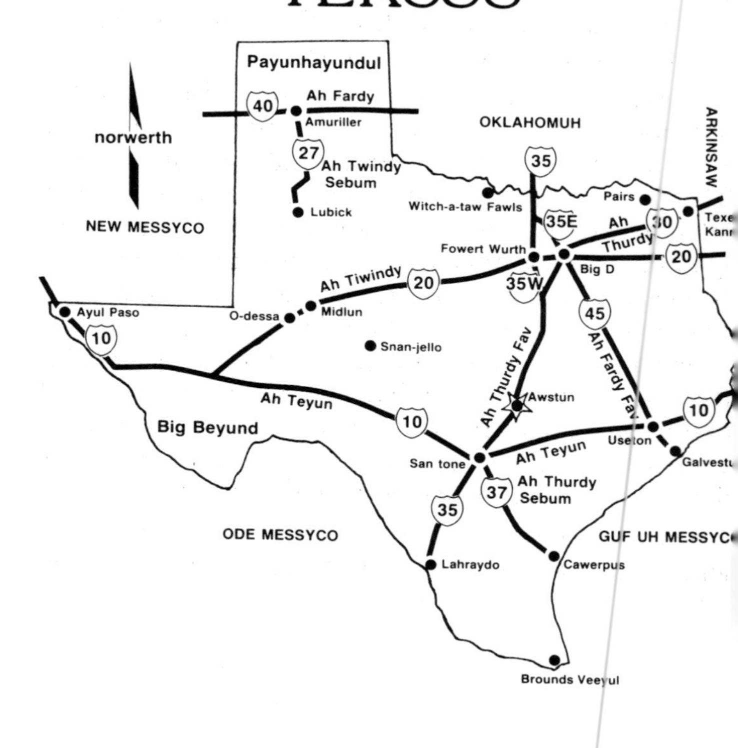

A (pronounced "aey")

Ah[1, 2] 1. the first person, singular
2. that portion of the anatomy with which one sees.
"Ah thank Ah got sumpn in mah ah" (1. I, 2. eye)

air [2] - 60 minutes.
"Ah monly drivin 50 mahls pur air." - (hour)

all [2] - 1. a liquid hydrocarbon which is produced from deep in the earth. 2. complete or whole. "Hid take all thuh all in Teksus tuh keep them Yankees warm thus winner." - (1. oil - not to be confused with the Southern pronunciation, "awl". 2. all)

Amerkin - citizen of the United States of America.
"Even Teksuns is Amerkins." - (American)

anavarsry - a repetitive celebration of a past occurence.
"Mah waf's gonna take may out tuh ate for our anavarsry." - (anniversary)

arncha - an inquiry concerning the addressee's plans.
"Arncha gunna go over tuh thuh pitchur sho tuhnite?" - (aren't you)

aukerd - clumsy, inept, embarrassing.
"Ah shore felt aukerd when thuh outhouse wall fayul down." - (awkward)

awf [1] - 1. a reduction or separation. 2. away from, at a distance. "Thet ¼-awf sayul is only 2 days awf." - (off)

B (pronounced "bay")

bawl - any toy which rolls and bounces.
"Thuh greatest game evur davised bah man is futbawl." - (ball)

Big D - the second largest city in Texas.
"The Cowboys is from Big D." - (Dallas)

bleeve [1] - to feel strongly about or to have faith in.
"Ah bleeve Earl Campbell iz thuh greatest futbawl player evur bornd." - (believe)

brayke - 1. to separate into pieces by force. 2. a device to stop motion.
"Few don't stop that Ah mona brayke yarm!" - (1. break, 2. brake)

breck - a masonry building material.
"Sum toms hay makes may so mad Ah could thow uh breck attum." - (brick)

C (pronounced "saey")

captul - the seat of government.
"Thuh Teksus Captul is thuh biggest in thuh whole, dang country." - (capitol, or capital)

cawdja - past tense of "cawya".
"Heard Joe cawdja last night. Whuddle say?" - (called you)

cawer - a 4-wheel vehicle normally used to transport people.
"Ah mona git may uh new diesel cawer." - (car)

chair - to yell or holler with gusto. "Her greatest desire is tuh bay uh chairleader." (cheer).

chard - area, usually green, around the house.
"Ah gotta mow mah frunt chard somtom." - (yard)

chayer - an article of furniture upon which to sit.
"Pull up thet ode chayer and set uhwahl." - (chair)

chur - second person, possessive.
"Wuzzat chur ode dawg tahd up ovare?" - (your)

churt - wearing apparel for the upper torso.
"Whardja git that funny lookin churt?" - (shirt)

code - opposite of hot.
"Ah gotta code in mah nose." - (cold)

cuz - normally comes before the reason.
"Ah didunt go ovur tuh town cuz Ah habumt got no money." - (because)

D (pronounced "daey")

defnutly - to be sure, without question. "Thets defnutly thuh smartest dawg in town." - (definitely)

diduhnit - a negative inquiry. "Diduhnit rain last night?" - (didn't it?)

difahkult - hard to do. "Hit's difahkult tuh walk and chew gum." - (difficult)

difernt - to distinguish between. "Thet red bawl slot difernt that thet blue bawl. - (different)"

dja - an affirmative inquiry. "Dja see thet game yester-dy?" - (did you) Note: some folks use "jew" or "didja".

dower - an opening in the wall through which one may walk. "Whut's behind thuh green dower?" - (door)

draimun - the act of having visions during sleep. "Ah must bay draimun!" - (dreaming)

drank [2] - to consume liquid. "Ah thank Ahl go down and havuh liddel drank." - (drink)

duduhnit - a positive inquiry. "Duduhnit feel good tuh win? - (doesn't it?)

dudunt - a contraction indicating the negative of the third person, singular verb form, do. "Ode Joe dudunt know witchin's up." - (doesn't)

E (pronounced "aee")

---

eevnun - the latter part of the day. "Thuh moon thuther eevnun wuz gist butiful." - (evening)

entahr - complete or universal; all of it. "Hay's thuh best goat roper hin thuh entahr warld!" - (entire)

eventchly - before long or ultimately. "Good will win out, eventchly." - (eventually)

evun - equal. "Them tew ode boys come out dead evun in thet race." - (even)

evurwonsinawhahl - periodically, but infrequently. "Ah git tuh drahv mah Pappa's pickup truk evurwonsinawhahl." - (ever once in a while)

F (pronounced "ayuf")

---

fahwar - the object or purpose of, or reason of action. "Wadja wonna go do that fahwar?" - (for) Note: also pronounced "fur" and "fuh" by well-meaning, but unenlightened Southerners.

faller - the opposite of lead. "Ahd faller her anywhare." - (follow)

far [1, 2] - the ignition of fuel from which to derive heat. "Thow sum lawgs on thet far." - (fire)

few - a qualified conjunction of the second person, singular. "Few kaynt spake thuh language, better not drank thuh warder." - (if you)

fergit - to lose recall of something. "Tuh err iz human; tuh fergit iz also human." - (forget)

figger - 1. the shape of human form. 2. to calculate. "Thet Cindy Lou shore has got uh fahn lookin figger." - (figure)

fixin [1] - preparing, getting ready. "Ode Joe's fixin tuh find himsef in uh heap uh trouble." - (fixing (to)

flare [1] - a blossum of a plant. "Thet yuller flare shore smayuls good." - (flower)

frayed - an affirmative or negative response. "Ahm frayed so." or "Ahm frayed not." - (afraid)

fraze - to render a material solid from temperature reduction. "Fah don't git mah coat Ah mona fraze!" - (freeze)

frunt - opposite of back. "Thuh cawer's out frunt." - (front)

G (pronounced "jey")

gittaholdayew - a Texas way to say "call you" or "contact" you. "Shay's sposed tuh gittaholdayew bout thet thus safternoon." - (get ahold of you)

gist - a word used by Texans and most Southerners to modify and strengthen others; or to buy time in the middle of a sentence to think of the right word. "Ah wuz gist so excited Ah could gist hardly stand it." - (just)

gitahwer - a stringed musical instrument used for pickin and grinnin. ''Thus hare's thuh best gitahwer Ahv evur strummed.'' - (guitar)

guesss - visitors. ''Ahl bet way hadda hunnert guesss at thuh wedden.'' - (guests)

guf - a large body of water for which a previously large and independent oil company was named. ''Thuh closest thang way got tuh un oshun iz thuh Guf uh Messyco.'' - (gulf)

gunna or **gonna** - a modifier which comes between the subject and the verb used to add emphasis, or to fill in and make the sentence sound right; used with third person. ''Hay's gunna git wet fee don't git outta thet rain.'' - (going (to)

H (pronounced ''aetch'')

---

ha - 1. upper elevation. 2. a state of inebriation. ''Thuh Mahl-Ha Stadyum iz in Denver.'' - (high)

habumt - a contraction to indicate the condition of not having. ''Ah habumt got uh dime tuh mah name.'' - (haven't)

hawh - signals message understood, but not worthy of additional comment; normally used alone. Note: if the syllable trails up it's a question. If not, a comment. ''Hawh!'' or ''Hawh?'' - (huh, ! or ?)

hidee - a unique form of greeting used almost exclusively by Texas Auggies; normally used alone, but echoed by other Aggies within earshot. "Hidee." "Hidee." - (how do you do)

hiduhnit - a negative inquiry. "Hiduhnit bout tom way headed home?" - (isn't it)

Hinyun - the original American. "Ah thank thuh cowboys sargunna git whipped by them Hinyuns thus tom." - (Indian; Note: never Injun!)

hyeru - a greeting, normally used alone and frequently answered, "Fahn, hyeru?" - (how are you?)

I (pronounced "ah")

I-O-no - used as an answer to virtually any question of a sub-teenager. "Whardja go tuhnight?" "I-O-no." "Whudja do?" "I-O-no." - (I don't know)

ignernt - without knowledge. "Ignernts of thuh law iz no excuse." - (ignorance)

innersekshun - the meeting of roads. "Joe Bob's place iz zakly thray mahls past thet innersekshun rot thare." - (intersection)

instudda - rather than. "Ahd ruthur hav thet great big bowl uh chili instudda thet liddel biddy un." - (instead of)

izit - the second part of many important questions. ''Whut izit?'' ''Who izit?'' - (is it?)

J (pronounced ''jay'')

janes - wearing apparel for the legs. ''Dja see them tot blue janes on thet whoamun?'' - (jeans)

jayul - a place of incarceration. ''Few keep runnin round with thet bunch yore gonna git thowed in jayul.'' - (jail)

jeyut - a fast airplane. ''Ah mona ketch may uh jeyut plane tuh Caleyfornyuh.'' - (jet)

joggerfee - the study of the Earth's surface. ''Ah made uh Bay-plus in Joggerfee.'' - (geography)

julry - rings, bracelets, necklaces. ''Thet whoamun gist luvs julry.'' - (jewelry)

K (pronounced ''kayee'')

Kang - the ruler or supreme authority. ''Thet guy thanks hay's Kang uv thuh warld.'' - (king)

kaynt - a contraction of can not. ''Ah gist kaynt wait til Christmas.'' - (can't)

kinduh - an approximation, or nearly. ''Ah now kinduh understaynd whut chur tawkin bout.'' - (kind of)

klane - not dirty or soiled. "Yew better klane up yore act." - (clean)

kliment - meteorological environment. "Few don't lahk Amuriller's kliment gist wait uh minent." - (climate)

kweyut - stop. "Yew better kweyut thet or Ahl slap yup sodda thuh hayud." - (quit)

L (pronounced "ayul")

---

lah - 1. a fib or untruth. 2. to recline. "Hit wuz gist uh liddel, wot lah." - (lie)

lahf - 1. the name of a magazine. 2. before death. "Ahv lived in Teksus most uv mah a-dult lahf." - (life)

lahk - 1. to enjoy. 2. to show affection. "Ah rilly do lahk yew, Betty Sue .. Ah do, Ah do!" - (like)

liberry - where books are housed. "Thay got lotsa books on how tuh tawk rot over at thuh liberry." - (library)

lot - an instrument or element which emits brightness. "Ah'd lahk tuh hayuv wunna them 60-watt lot bubs, playze. - (light)

M (pronounced ''eyum'')

mahsef - one's own self. ''... and Ah sayud tuh mahsef, 'Sef, yew kaynt git by with thet.' '' - (myself)

mahtearyul - what a thing is made of. ''Sumtoms Johnny Carson dudunt have very good mahtearyul, but hay still tawks funny.'' - (material)

mawce - a parasitic growth on trees. ''Thet mawce on them trays shore makes hit scary.'' - (moss)

mawl - a center, normally covered, used for shopping. Keep them wimmen away from thuh mawl.'' - (mall)

minent - 60 seconds. ''Ahl bay thare in uh New York minent.'' - (minute)

mona - used with the first person, singular to state what one intends to do. ''Ah mona git mahsef uh brand new fishin poe.'' - (going to; see ''gonna'' or ''gunna'' for second and third person)

N (pronounced ''eyun'')

n-sod - within a building or room, or other enclosure. ''Izzat ode Slim n-sod thet bildun?'' - (inside)

naw - a negative response. ''Dja git paid tuhday?'' ''Naw.'' ''Tuhmorrow?'' ''Naw.'' - (no) Note: sometimes pronounced ''naugh''.

nuthun - the opposite of something. "Wheyun yew duhvide nuthun by sumpm yew git nuthun." - (nothing)

O (pronounced "oh")

---

o-cheut - an exclamatory expletive, generally considered to be equal to 10 "ATTABOYS". Normally used alone. - (aw come on now, say it slowly)

ode - ancient. "Thuh ode gray mare shay ain't whut shay ustuh bay." - (old)

opsit - completely different. "Thay say opsits attrack." - (opposite)

ovare - indicating a place or location. "Put thet liddel chayer rot ovare." - (over there)

P (pronounced "pay")

---

pahn - an evergreen indiginous to Texas. "Thuh Big Thicket's gist plumb full uh Pahn trays." - (pine)

paypul [2] - human beings. "Teksuns iz thuh greatest paypul in thuh whole warld." - (people)

pears - a statement of apparent observation. "Pears tuh may yore puttin on uh liddel weight." - (it) appears)

pickchur or **pitchur** - a reproduction of the original. "Ah mona take uh pitchur with mah Instuhmatik." (picture; both pronunciations used in Texas)

pillar - a soft object placed under one's head. "Way ustuh have pillar fites when way wuz liddel kids." - (pillow)

playze - a polite request. "Brang may uh cup uh coffee, playze." - (please)

preshate - to express gratitude. "Ah shore preshate yawl brangin thuh beer." - (appreciate)

probly - a modifier of limited certainty. "Hit's probly not gonna rain tuhday, either." - (probably)

purdy - 1. a degree of beauty. 2. a degree of completeness. "Shay shore iz purdy." "Ah feel purdy good tuhday." - (pretty)

Q (pronounced "kew")

Note: I have never ever heard a Texan pronounce a word beginning with the letter "Q" - lots of "KW's", but no "Q's". For example, a "kwane" is a female leader.

R (pronounced "aruh")

rang [2] - 1. the present tense sound made by a bell. 2. jewelry for the fingers. "Gist gimme uh rang when yore reddy tuh go." - (ring)

reeyul - an adjective expressing conviction or magnitude. "Thet warder iz reeyul hard." - (real)

rilly [2] - another form of "reeyul". "Thet chikun rilly duz smayul good." - (really)

rot - 1. the opposite of left. 2. correct. "Yew gist go down thet road till yew git tuh thuh fowerk, then take uh rot turn." - (right)

S (pronounced "ayus")

sahn - an indicator or director or information conveyor. "Them ducks flyin north izza sahn of Sprang." - (sign)

Santone - a major city in south central Texas where the Alamo is located. "Shay's mah Santone rose." - (San Antonio)

Saowth - that portion of the United States below the Mason-Dixon line, including Texas. "Hain't nuthun wrong with anybody whut comes from the Saowth." - (South)

sayud - past tense of "say". "Yew hurd whut Ah sayud, yew ain't dayuf." - (said)

sayul - 1. normally referring to a drastic reduction in price. 2. that which captures the wind on a certain type of boat by the same name. "Ah bought thet purdy red hat on sayul." (1. sale 2. sail, and sometimes 3. sell)

skoo - the place of learning. "Few don't hurry yore gunna bay late fahwer skoo." - (school)

skrane - a cover for windows to let in wind but keep out everything else. "Dja see thet big skeeter crawl thoo thet hole in thuh skrane?" - (screen)

smahl - a pleasant expression on one's face. "Smahl and thuh whole warld smahls with yew." - (smile)

smatter - the object of inquiries about one's health or condition. "Whut smatter witchew, boy?" - (what is the matter)

smayul - an emission of fragrance. "Whutzat smayuls so bayud?" or "Skunks smayul tarbul!" - (smell)

speshuly - particularly. "Git them pigs in thet pen, speshuly thet big un." - (especially)

sprankul - a light rain. "Looks lahk hit's gunna pucker up and sprankul in uh minent." - (sprinkle)

sumoze - to indicate which and how many. "Ahl have sumoze jelly beans ovare, playze." - (some of those)

sumpn - an article or item or object. "Thar's sumpn bout un Aqua Velva man." - (something)

T (pronounced "tay")

tah - 1. to intertwine rope or string in an orderly fashion. 2. a dead heat. 3. men's wearing apparel for the neck. "Thonly thang worsun uh tah izza loss." - (tie)

tarbul - awful or dreadful. "Hit's been uh tarbul code winner." - (terrible)

tawk - verbal communications. "Sum paypul shore tawk funny." - (talk)

tayul - 1. a story not lacking embellishment (Texans like these kind of stories). 2. nature's signal that a passing animal has passed. "Teksuns iz node fur thur tahl tayuls." - (1. tale, 2. tail)

tayvay - an electronic video receiving instrument. "Ah got uh short in mah tayvay." - (TV)

thang [2] - an object. "Sum thangs are gist meant tuh bay." - (thing)

thayure - a place or location. "Put thet sack down rot thayure." - (there)

thuh - principle modifier of nouns, an artical. "Thuh rain in Teksus falls mainly on thuh coastal plain."

Note: - Texans almost always spell the previous word properly but hardly ever pronounce it right. (the)

thur - third person, possessive. "Thet's thur house ovare." - (their)

tode [2] - past tense of tell. "Hif Ah tode yew once Ah tode yew uh hunnert toms." - (told)

tom [2] - the hour of the day. "Whut tom izit?" - (time)

tray - a large, growing plant. "Ah thank Ahl nevur say uh thang as purdy azza tray." - (tree)

tuh - a direction or a place, or an adverb, but never a number or "also". "Yew gunna go all thuh way tuh Dallus in thet ode truk?" - (to)

U (pronounced "yew")

u-betcha - an affirmative comment, normally used alone. "Dja git paid tuhday?" "U-betcha!" -(no known English phrase connotes the exact meaning of this term)

uh-hawh or **uh-huh** - an affirmative response normally used alone. (example sentence above could be answered with this term)

Useton - the largest city in Texas. "Useton's thuh all captul uv thuh warld." - (Houston)

ustuh - expresses when in the past an act was or was not performed. "Way shore ustuh hav uh lottuh fun going tuh thuh Teksus-OU game." - (used to)

V (pronounced "vay")

vahlayshun - an act against the law. "Parkin next tuh uh yeller curb izza vahlayshun." - (violation)

viktray - a triumph. "Gimme viktray, or gimme dayuth." - (victory)

vurchully - essentially, or almost all. "Vurchully evur Teksun izza Dallus Cowboy fayun." - (virtually)

W (pronounced "dubya" or "dubyou")

waf - a female spouse. "Thet's un ode waf's tayul." - (wife)

war [1] - 1. a strand of metallic fiber. 2. a colloquial term for a telegram. "They's not uh cow been bornd whut can brayke thoo uh strang uh bob-war." - (wire)

warder - H_20. "How ha's thuh warder, Captun?" - (water)

wartch - to cleanse. "Ah mona wartch out mah coffee cup." - (wash)

wayul - 1. the beginning of nearly every Texan's sentence. 2. a hole dug to recover a subsurface resource. "Wayul, hifit don't rain thus week, that creek's gunna bay plumb dry." - (well)

Wayust - the opposite of East. "Fowert Wurth's whar thuh Wayust begins." - (West)

wender - the opening in a wall to let in breeze and light. "Put uh candle in yore wender ..." - (window)

wha - an inquiry as to the cause or reason. "Now, wha dja go out an play in thet mud?" - (why)

whale - a round object which normally rolls and turns. "Few been drankin, don't take thuh whale." - (wheel)

whayer - an adverb to describe an unknown place. "Whayer dja git they funny lookin hat?" - (where)

whoamun - the female of the Human species. "Shay's uh hard hardud whoamun ...." - (woman)

whut - something which is normally not known. "Ah don't know whut yore tawkin bout." - (what)

wonna - a verb expressing one's desire. "Playze Mister Custer, Ah don't wonna go." - (want to)

Y (pronounced "why")

---

y-ahlbdayumd - an exclamatory comment normally used alone. - (not worthy of additional elaboration)

y-oncha - a personal suggestion. "Y-oncha go ovur tuh thuh fillin stayshun tuh git sum gayus?" - (why don't you)

yawl [1, 2] - the collective second person, singular, never "you-all". "Yawl kumbak now, yuh hear?" (a unique Southern word)

yayus or **yayuh** or **yayup** - an affirmative response, frequently used alone; sometimes prefaced with "Hayul". - (yes)

yew - second person, singular. "Yew hain't nuthun but uh houndawg ...." - (you)

Z (pronounced "zaey")

---

zekatuv - A corporate or business leader. "Thet good lookin liddel secretary's whut Ah call uh zekatuv sweet." - (executive)

zatrot - an inquiring comment indicating message understood, but not totally believed; normally used alone and followed by an affirmative response like, "uh-huh". - (is that right)

THE DAYS AND THE MONTHS ....

SUNDY ....Sunday
MUNDY ....Monday
CHEWSDY ....Tuesday
WINSDY ....Wednesday
THURSDY ....Thursday
FRYDY ....Friday
SADDERDY ....Saturday

JANYAWARY ....January
FEBBERYAWARY or FEBBERWARY
....February
MARTCH ....March
ABRUL ....April
MAEY ....May
DJOON ....June
DJOOLIE ....July
AWG-GHUST ....August
CEPTIMBUR ....September
OKTOBUR ....October
NOVEYUMBUR ....November
DECEYUMBUR ....December

AND THE NUMBERS ....

WUN	- 1	1st	FURSD
TEW	- 2	2nd	SEKUNT
THRAY	- 3	3rd	THURD
FOWER	- 4	4th	FOWERTH
FAV	- 5	5th	FIFD
SICKS	- 6	6th	SICKSED
SEBUM	- 7	7th	SEBUMTHD
ATE	- 8	8th	ATHD
NAHN	- 9	9th	NONTH
TEYUN	- 10	10th	TEYUNTH
LEBUM	-11		
TWAYULV	- 12		
THURTANE	- 13		
FORTANE	- 14		
FIFTANE	- 15		
SICKSTANE	- 16		
SEBUMTANE	- 17		
A-TANE	- 18		
NONTANE	19		
TWINDY	20		
THURDY	- 30		
FARDY	- 40		
FIFDY	- 50		
SICKSDY	- 60		
SEBUMDY	- 70		
ADY	- 80		
NONDY	- 90		
*HUNDURT	- 100		
**THOUSUNT	- 1000		

* 101 and there - after pronounced "HUNNERD"

** 1001 and thereafter is pronounced "THOUSUN"

.... AND, THE COLORS

RED	RAYUD	(1)
BLUE	BULLOO	(2)
GREEN	GRANE	(3)
YELLOW	YELLER	
ORANGE	ARNJUH	(4)
PURPLE	BURPEL	(5)
WHITE	WOT	(6)
TAN	TAYUN	
BLACK	BLAAK	(10)
BROWN	BRAOYONE	
PINK	PANK	
MAROON	MROONE	(7)
GREY	GRAEY	(11)
GOLD	GODE	(8)
SILVER	SEEYULVUR	(9)

DARKER	DAWERKER
LIGHTER	LAHTER
BRIGHTER	BROTTER
SOFTER	SOWFTUR

(see next page for a definition of seemingly peculiar methods of communicating about one's alma mater by calling out its colors; refer to codes above for quick reference.)

"COLOR TAWK"

In the event you overhear some Texan mention a couple of colors, like, "Nuthin's tew good fawer Thuh Mroone 'n Wot....", chances are that individual is talking about his favorite team. there are many peculiar combinations of colors with which the idle observer should be generally familiar in order to communicate. some of these are (reference colors on previous page):

(7) & (6) - Texas A&M, also known as TEKSUS AGGIES, or FARMERS, and by some other names (A&M).

(4) & (6) - The University of Texas, or TEKSUS, also known variably as "Thuh Horns" or "TEASIPS", or "Steers", or sometimes by the proper name, the "LONGHORNS" (UT - Austin).

(3) & (8) - Baylor University, also known as the "THE BAYURS" (Bears), or the Babtusses (Baptists), [who now know how to dance]. (BU)

(1) & (2) - Southern Methodist University, also known as the "PONIES" OR "SMOO", or more recently by somewhat less flattering terms. (SMU) Interestingly, however, with the recent introduction of the Big 12 to Texas, these colors also represent the "JAYHAWKS" or "them dang birds" from Kansas, which isn't all that important until you start playing "roundball". (KU)

(1) & (6) - Used to be either the University of Houston, or the University of Arkansas (you could normally tell which just by looking at who's talking).

In the case of UH, you may also hear "COOGS" or "COOGEROOS" or "BAYOU BUNNIES". (UH) If it's U of A, sometimes you'd also hear "HAWGS" or "PORKERS", generally preceded by something sounding like "Sooooooeeee Pig". (U of A) [now in the SEC, and therefore officially exhumed from Texas lore].. However, now that the Big 12 cometh, one also has to consider the University of Nebraska, "HUSKERS" or "BIG RED", or the inimitable Sooners of the University of Oklahoma, although they insist that their (1) & (6) is really Crimson and Cream (what do they know?). The latter is especially noted by the fact that their fight song has only two words...*no commentary intended.* (NU and OU)

(1) & (10) - Texas Tech University, or the "RAYUD RAIDURS", or sometimes referred to as the "PLAINS BANDITS". (TT, or Tech)

(5) & (6) - Used to be solely Texas Christian University, or the "FROGS" or the "TOADS", or something even less romantic. (TCU) However, we have now discovered another institution represented by the same color combination - namely Kansas State University, which may or may not be a significant displacement of the noted place in history garnered by the Horn Toads of Fowert Wurth. (KSU) [*there are some visitors who insist that K-State's colors are really (5) & (9)*].

(2) & (11) - Rice University, or the "ROSSOLS", or "Thuh Boys Frum Thuh Instatoot". (R) [*of course, everybody knows the best representatives of this great institution is the "MOB" - i.e., the "Marching Owl Band".*]

(9) & (2) - The Cowboys, of Dallas - frequently World Champions, and on everybody's 'most deposed' lists. (★).

(2) - As in "LUV YA (2)", the Oilers, formerly of Houston, but now from somewhere in Tennessee.

There are an infinite number of other color combinations spoken perhaps somewhat less frequently by Texans than those listed above. However, I have neither the time, space, nor the energy to compile these here. You just have to learn *that Teksuns hayuv vary colorful spaetch.*

GETTING AROUND TEXAS...

There are a bunch of places in Texas that have names that you think you'll be able to spell and find on a map...but, you won't be able to. Due in part to Texas' colorful history, and the fact that most Texans can't spell very well and they talk funnier than they spell, there are some peculiar ways they have chosen to spell and pronounce the names of some of their respective towns. Following is a brief list of places that you're likely to hear about, spelled the way you think they should be, and then the way Texans spell them, and roughly where they are. A few more Texas towns are shown on the map in front.

"Ana-whack" - *Anahuac* - across the bay from Baytown.

"Bernie" - *Boerne* - on I-10 about 20 miles from San Antonio.

"Clayburn" - *Cleburne* - on U.S. 67 southwest of Dallas.

"Uless" - *Euless* - East of Dallas - part of "HEB", Hurst, Euless, Bedford.

"Gothwait" - *Goldwaithe* - on U.S. 84 West of Waco.

"Grossback" - *Groesbeck* - on TX 164 East of Waco.

"Green" - *Gruene* - just southwest of New Braunfels.

"Hi" - *Hye* - on U.S. 290 West of Johnson City.

"Hilund" - *High Island* - the area along the coast between the Boliver peninsula and the Texas-Louisiana state line, south of Winnie.

"Hello-tis" - *Helotes* - outside of San Antonio towards the Hill Country.

"Iryann" - *Iraan* - on U.S. 190 East of Bakersfield.

"Curns" - *Kerens* - on TX 31 East of Corsicana (not unlike Behrens, for "Burns").

"Clean" - *Killeen* - on U.S. 190 West of Temple.

"Manshack" - *Manchaca* - South of Austin.

"Maheya" - *Mexia* - on U.S. 84 West of Waco.

"Floogerville" - *Pflugerville* - North of Austin.

"Far" - *Pharr* - in the Valley between McAllen and Harlingen on US 83.

"Refurio" - *Refugio* - on U.S. 77 North of Corpus Christi.

"Sprang" - *Spring* - North of Houston on I-45.

"Welder" - *Waelder* - on I-10 East of San Antonio.

"Walksahatchee" - *Waxahachie* - on I-35E, South of Dallas (home of the former Super Collider).

"Whymer" - *Weimar* - between Houston and San Antonio on I-10.

This is by no means an unabridged listing. It is just to give you some of the "flavor". You'll hear some more....lots more!

A LITTLE TEXAS "CULTURE"

There is a custom of Texans and other southwesterners that is sometimes a little bit unnerving for our out-of-state visitors. It's the good, old-fashioned WAVE *(not the football stadium variety).* It can be seen at any time, but mostly from an approaching driver, generally in rural Texas. Of course, most Texans are naturally friendly and they enjoy greeting visitors. But, there are sometimes a number of other subtle messages being given when a passing motorist waves at you. Generally, a wave means the opposing driver is indicating that he or she is mostly awake and things down the road on their side are pretty much OK.

There are several versions of acceptable waves in Texas. Some are:

(1) *1- or 2-finger wave*: This is either from a lazy Texan or one who has all he can handle just holding on to the steering wheel, but still wants to be friendly. Any combination of fingers is an acceptable wave in Texas, regardless of possible connotations elsewhere.

(2) *full-hand, straight-arm wave*: This form of wave is often given by former Marine sergeants or football coaches. It's a subtle way of stating, "I'm waving because of convention, but I'm in full charge of my half of the road."

(3) *the four-fingered "piccolo-playing" wave*: This is kind of a sissy wave for Texans. Upon investigation, you'll likely find most of these wavers aren't.

(4) *the half-hearted 2-finger salute wave*: Often these wavers have served time in the military, or know somebody who has, or they're adjusting their hat and you just think they're waving.

(5) *the full-handed, 60-degree rotational wave*: I always think these folks are trying to get a fly or a bee out of the vehicle. May be.

(6) *the out-the-window, full hand wave*: Check this one closely. He may actually be trying to tell you something...or, he may be grabbing bugs.

School Waves: Several Texas educational institutions have their own unique or *peculiar* waves or signals. For example:

UT - 1st and 4th fingers vertical, rest held to the palm with the thumb ("Hook 'Em Horns").

Texas A&M - thumb vertical, fingers in a fist ("Gig 'Em Aggies").

Texas Tech - thumb vertical, 1st finger out at 90-degrees, other fingers in fist (shape of a finger pistol) ("Ride 'Em Raiders").

Baylor - a hand "claw", often accompanied with a growl.

U of Houston - 3rd finger held to the palm with thumb.

Of course, there are several other kinds of waves for various institutions, clubs, etc., some of which aren't necessarily sanctioned. For example, oftentimes you'll see the UT wave (above) given upside-down (horns down). That generally indicates that the waver's institution is playing UT that week. It is used indiscriminately by alums or friends of several institutions, mostly out-of-state, but none of those listed above.

A Teksus tip of the hat to all y'all.

ABOUT THE AUTHOR....

Ode Keyun iz uh naytuv Teksun whoo ayus leyuved eyun thuh grayte stayte uv O-lawhomuh fur mohst uv heyus aey-duhit lahf. Hit idunt hurtum, but heeze ahlwaze hayud uh sauft pod eyun heyus hewart fur ahl thoze fahn fokes hoo kudunt hundurstayund whut hay wuz sayun. oh, hay duidud tuh rot thus liddel bukleht tuh hep m.

(Old Ken is a native Texan who has lived in e great state of Oklahoma for most of his adult fe. It didn't hurt him, but he's always had a soft oot in his heart for all those fine folks who couldn't nderstand what he was saying. So, he decided to rite this little booklet to help them.)

NOTES